How to Create Language Experts With
Literary Terms

Codi Hrouda and Emma McInerney
with Lyle Lee Jenkins

My Book of Similes and Metaphors

By: _____

School: _____

Teacher: _____

Date: _____

My Book of Analyzing a Character

By: _____

School: _____

Teacher: _____

Date: _____

My Book of Comparing and Contrasting Literary Text

By: _____

School: _____

Teacher: _____

Date: _____

My Book of Main Idea and Key Details

By: _____

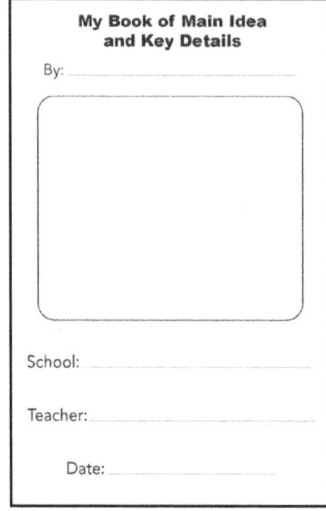

School: _____

Teacher: _____

Date: _____

My Book of Judging Actual Events

By: _____

School: _____

Teacher: _____

Date: _____

Perfect School Collection™

To contact the authors regarding keynotes, workshops or bulk orders, visit LtoJ.net/Contact

ISBN: 978-1-956457-69-8

Book Design & Graphics: Christy Courtright, Christy's Customs LLC
Quality Assurance Manager: Kelly Lippert
Publishing Consultant: Martha Bullen, Bullen Publishing Services
Distribution Coordinator: Maggie McLaughlin

Printed in the United States of America

The Perfect School Collection™

How to Create a Perfect School by Lyle Lee Jenkins
How to Create a Perfect Home School by Lyle Lee Jenkins and Kelly Hawkinson Lippert

Perfect School Collection™ Resources

How to Create Math Experts series by Peggy McLean and Lyle Lee Jenkins
How to Create Math Experts with Fluency Quizzes by Peggy McLean and Lyle Lee Jenkins
How to Create Math Experts with Math Standards Quizzes by Peggy McLean, Laura Hayes and Lyle Lee Jenkins
How to Create a Math Foundation for Future Math Experts by Lyle Lee Jenkins
How to Create Bible Experts: Genesis to Revelation by Richard Douglas Junior Jenkins with Lyle Lee Jenkins

Early Readers

Bible Patterns for Young Readers series by Lyle Lee Jenkins
Aesop Patterns for Young Readers series by Lyle Lee Jenkins

Young Authors

Wordless Books for Young Authors series by Jim Chansler and Lyle Lee Jenkins

Special Project

All About Henry: Rich Widower of Savannah Valley by Lyle Lee Jenkins

CONTENTS

INTRODUCTION

The philosophy behind these booklets is that they are student-led, and elementary (K - 6) standards driven. In other words, students can independently complete much of the materials they are expected to learn in school with occasional pre-teaching.

The booklets are designed with a left-brain/right-brain balance. The back cover is a right-brain activity and the inside pages are clearly left-brain. The page prior to each grade level gives parents and teachers background knowledge and suggestions to successfully support their students and children through the booklets.

In order to create and assemble the booklets, parents and teachers can scan the QR code provided at the end of the book to download digital copies. To ensure proper printing, please utilize double sided printing and set your printer to "flip" on the short edge. The front page will be the front and back cover of the booklet. We have also included some bonus booklets within this series to support additional literary term exploration.

Enjoy,

Codi Hrouda, Emma McInerney and Lyle Lee Jenkins

GRADE 4
BOOKLET DIRECTIONS

My Book of Similes and Metaphors:
Students may need to be pre-taught similes and metaphors. Access to texts with examples of similes and metaphors and coloring supplies will be needed for this booklet.

My Second Book of Prefixes and Suffixes:
Students may need to have access to books that contain prefixes and suffixes.

My Book of Homographs:
Students may need to be pre-taught homographs. Access to a non-fiction book and coloring supplies will be needed for this booklet.

My Book of Analyzing a Character:
Students may need to be pre-taught character traits. Access to a fiction book and coloring supplies will be needed for this booklet.

My Book of Comparing and Contrasting Literary Texts:
Students will need to have access to fiction books.

My Book of Summary and Theme:
Students will need to have access to books and coloring supplies.

My Book of Inferences Using Evidence:
Students will need to have access to books and coloring supplies.

My Book of Main Idea and Key Details:
Students may need to be pre-taught main idea and key details. Access to non-fiction books will be needed for this booklet.

My Book of Judging Actual Events:
Students will need to have access to a historical fiction and non-fiction book on the same topic.

My Book of Onomatopoeias:
Students may need to be pre-taught onomatopoeias. Access to a graphic novel or comic strip and coloring supplies will be needed for this booklet.

Choose a metaphor and simile from books you are reading or from the previous page and draw a picture and write what each example means.

Simile

Metaphor

Either

My Book of Similes and Metaphors

By: _____

School: _____

Teacher: _____

Date: _____

Simile - a comparison of two things using the words "like" or "as".

Metaphor - a comparison of two things that does NOT use the words "like" or "as".

Read the sentences below and mark them as a smilie or a metaphor.

The classroom was a zoo.
◊ Simile   ◊ Metaphor

Her smile is like sunshine.
◊ Simile   ◊ Metaphor

He was as busy as a beaver.
◊ Simile   ◊ Metaphor

My computer is an old dinosaur.
◊ Simile   ◊ Metaphor

Alex's bedroom is as cold as ice.
◊ Simile   ◊ Metaphor

She is a night owl.
◊ Simile   ◊ Metaphor

Read books and list any examples of similes and metaphors.

Similes   Metaphors

Student booklets are available via the QR code at the end of the book

As you read, list words with the prefixes and suffixes you have learned in this booklet.

_____ _____

_____ _____

_____ _____

_____ _____

_____ _____

_____ _____

_____ _____

_____ _____

My Second Book of Prefixes and Suffixes

By: _____

School: _____

Teacher: _____

Date: _____

Use the definitions to fill in the correct prefix for each word.

In- / Im-: Not
Anti-: Against
De-: Remove
Dis-: Not

_____agree

_____rail

_____slavery

_____obey

_____able

_____social

_____possible

_____compose

_____flate

_____honest

Rewrite each word using the correct suffix.
Remember some base words may need to be changed.

-ly: Characteristic of
    Adding -ly changes an adjective to an adverb
-able /-ible: can be done
-ment: action or process
-ful: full of

_____ _____
(reverse)   (slow)

_____ _____
(change)   (amaze)

_____ _____
(lone)   (pain)

_____ _____
(wonder)   (sink)

_____ _____
(disappoint)   (discuss)

Student booklets are available via the QR code at the end of the book

Write a homograph pair.
Draw a picture and write a sentence using both words.

Homograph 1 | Homograph 2

My Book of Homographs

By: _____

School: _____

Teacher: _____

Date: _____

Homographs - words that are spelled the same but have different pronunciations and meanings.
Example: Tear (cry) and Tear (rip)

Draw pictures and write sentences using the two meanings of the homograph below:

BOW

Write a sentence for each homograph to show both meanings.

Bass
Sentence 1:

_____

Sentence 2:

_____

Close
Sentence 1:

_____

Sentence 2:

_____

Student booklets are available via the QR code at the end of the book

List traits of a person in your life. Provide evidence (words, actions) to support their traits.

_____
Name

Words:

Actions:

Traits with Evidence:

_____

_____

_____

_____

My Book of Analyzing a Character

By: _____

School: _____

Teacher: _____

Date: _____

Read a fictional story and collect evidence to identify the character's strongest traits.

Thoughts:

Words:

Actions:

Using the evidence on the previous page, list as many character traits that apply to the character using complete sentences.
Give the best evidence for each character unit.

_____

_____

_____

_____

_____

_____

_____

_____

_____

_____

Student booklets are available via the QR code at the end of the book

Write a story that has both similar and different literary elements as your favorite tall tale.

_____

_____

_____

_____

_____

_____

_____

_____

_____

My Book of Comparing and Contrasting Literary Text

By: _____

School: _____

Teacher: _____

Date: _____

Read two fiction books and compare and contrast the literary elements
(characters, setting, conflict, plot, and theme)

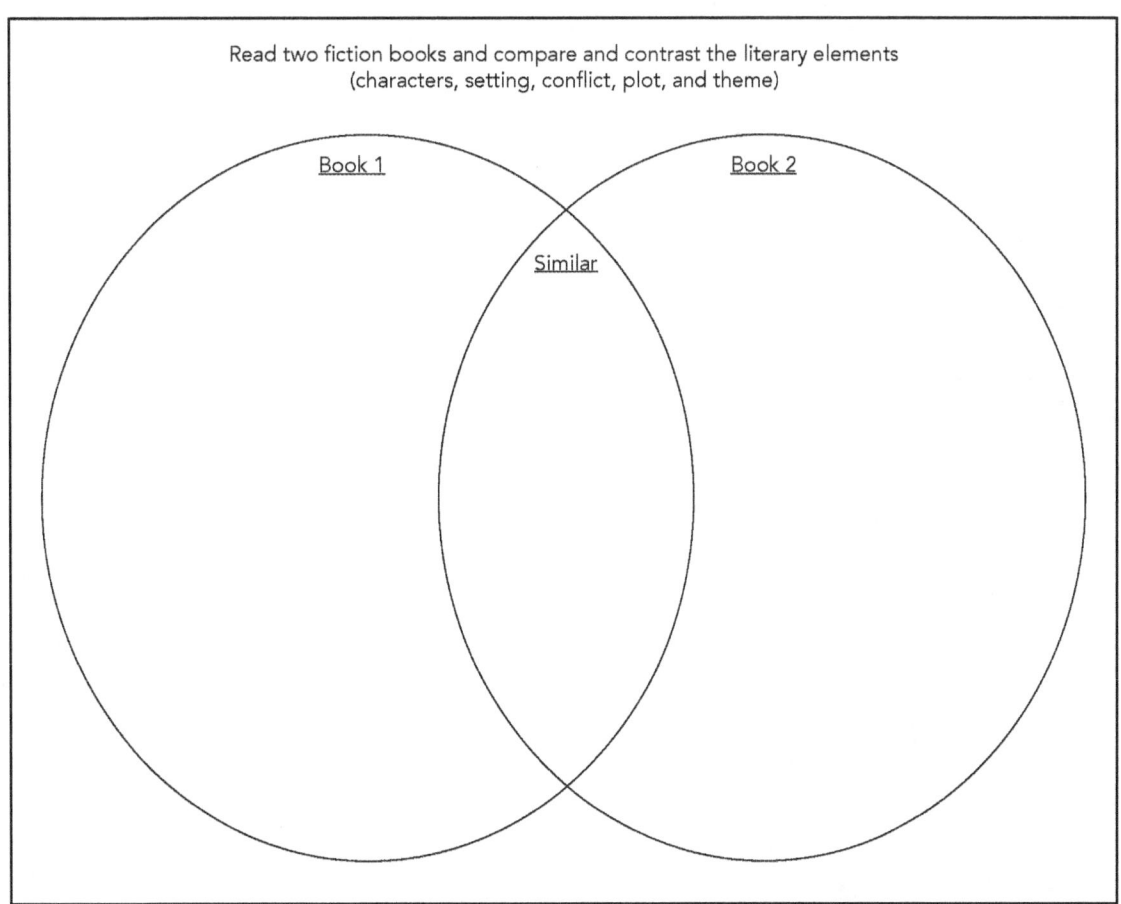

Book 1

Book 2

Similar

Student booklets are available via the QR code at the end of the book

Write a story that has both similarities and differences in its summary and theme as a favorite book.

My Book of Summary and Theme

By: _____

School: _____

Teacher: _____

Date: _____

_____

Summary - retells the main events of a story in a shorter version.

Theme - a message or lesson from the story that you can apply to your own life.

Read a fictional book. Write a summary using the chart below. Then complete the theme.

Somebody	Wanted	But	So	Then

The theme of the story is...

_____

_____

_____

Student booklets are available via the QR code at the end of the book

Create a series of pictures to tell a story. Be sure the pictures have enough detail for the reader to identify the problem and solution.

My Book of Inferences Using Evidence

By: _____

School: _____

Teacher: _____

Date: _____

Read two fiction books and explain how the character in each book responded to the challenges they faced.

_____ Title of Book 1	_____ Title of Book 2
Inference:	Inference:
Evidence:	Evidence:
Inference:	Inference:
Evidence:	Evidence:

Pretend you are writing a book about your life thus far. Provide the main idea and key details that would best describe your life.

My Book of Main Idea and Key Details

By: _____

Main Idea:

_____

_____

_____

_____

Key Details:

1. _____

_____

2. _____

_____

3. _____

_____

School: _____

Teacher: _____

Date: _____

Main Idea - What the text is mostly about.

Key Detail - Facts or examples that tell more about the main idea.

Read two fiction books and explain how the character in each book responded to the challenges they faced.

Title of Book 1	Title of Book 2

Main Idea:

_____

_____

_____

Main Idea:

_____

_____

_____

Key Details:

1. _____

2. _____

3. _____

Key Details:

1. _____

2. _____

3. _____

Student booklets are available via the QR code at the end of the book

Read a non-fiction book and collect facts about the topic. Once you have collected the facts, write a literary story with related events/facts.

_____

_____

_____

_____

_____

_____

_____

_____

_____

My Book of Judging Actual Events

By: _____

School: _____

Teacher: _____

Date: _____

Read a literary and a non-fiction book on the same topic. In the chart below, fill in events/facts as you read. Once you are done reading, cross out any **literary** events/facts that were not repeated in the non-fiction book.

Literary Book Title	Non-Fiction Book Title

Tell a story using a comic strip.
Make sure to include several onomatopoeias.

My Book of Onomatopoeias

By: _____

School: _____

Teacher: _____

Date: _____

Onomatopoeia - words that sound like the object they name or the sound those objects make.

Read a graphic novel or comic strip and list the onomatopoeias you find:

Circle the words that are examples of onomatopoeias:

Firework	Hee - Haw
Zipper	Snake
Choo Choo	Chomp
Pound	Boom
Slurp	Fan
Pow	Drop

_____ _____

_____ _____

_____ _____

_____ _____

_____ _____

_____ _____

_____ _____

CONTINUE CREATING LITERARY EXPERTS

BONUS BOOKLETS

A quick internet search for literary terms brings up hundreds of words. In addition, there are many topics to study as students gain more meaning from language and increase their writing skills.

Thus, the following blank pages are designed for students to write additional booklets about literary terms not included in *How to Create Language Experts with Literary Terms*. After selecting a new term, students select the format that best fits the task of writing about the literary term or concept.

There are times when children become so engrossed with a particular term that they want to make their booklet larger. These blank pages can also be used to add to existing booklets included in *How to Create Language Experts with Literary Terms*.

Student booklets are available via the QR code at the end of the book

---

My Book of _____

By: _____

School: _____

Teacher: _____

Date: _____

Title of Book 1

Title of Book 2

Student booklets are available via the QR code at the end of the book

My art:

Student booklets are available via the QR code at the end of the book

Book 1 Title: _____   Book 2 Title: _____

Book Title

Book Title

Student booklets are available via the QR code at the end of the book

Read two books and compare and contrast a literary element
(characters, setting, conflict, plot, and theme)

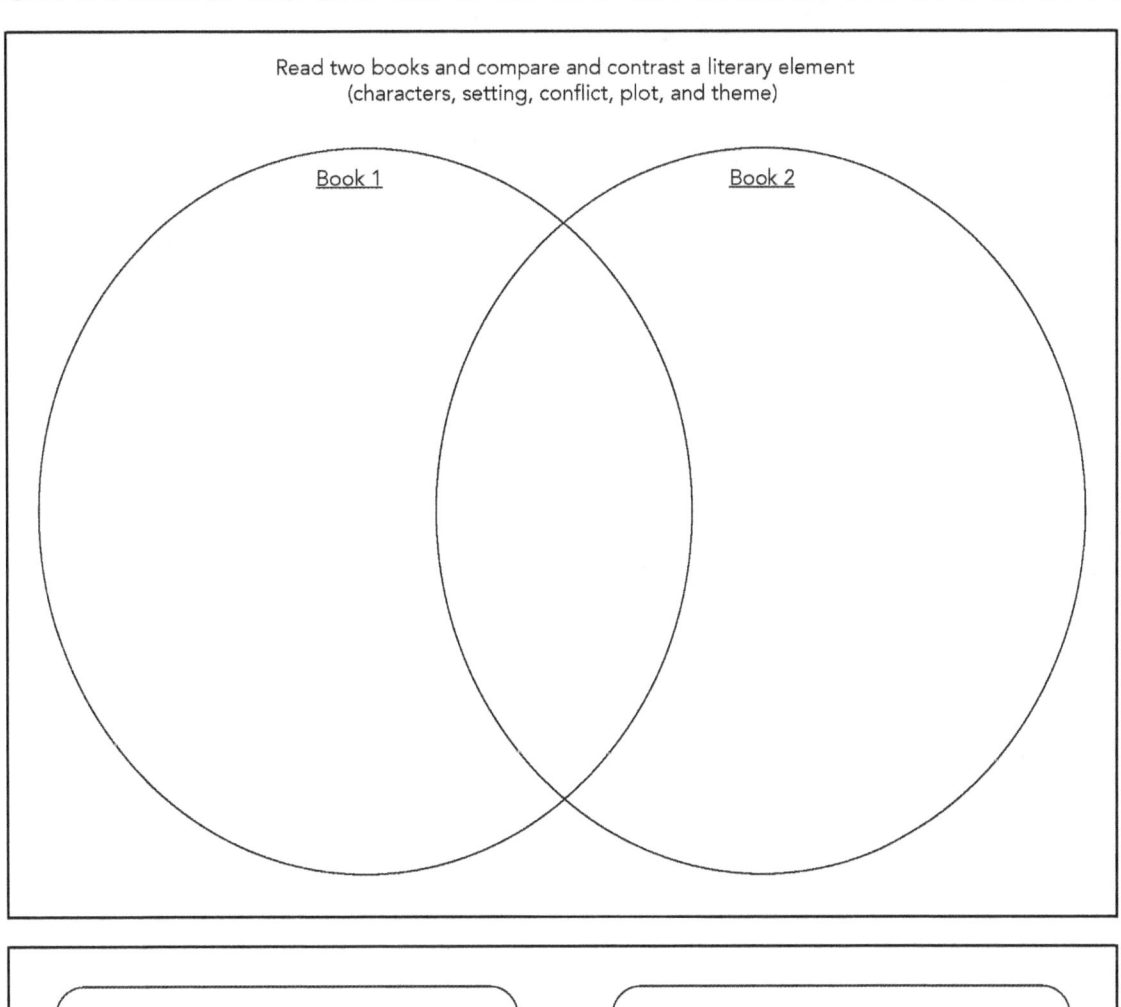

Book 1

Book 2

Student booklets are available via the QR code at the end of the book

---

Book Title

Book Title

Title of Book One

Title of Book Two

Student booklets are available via the QR code at the end of the book

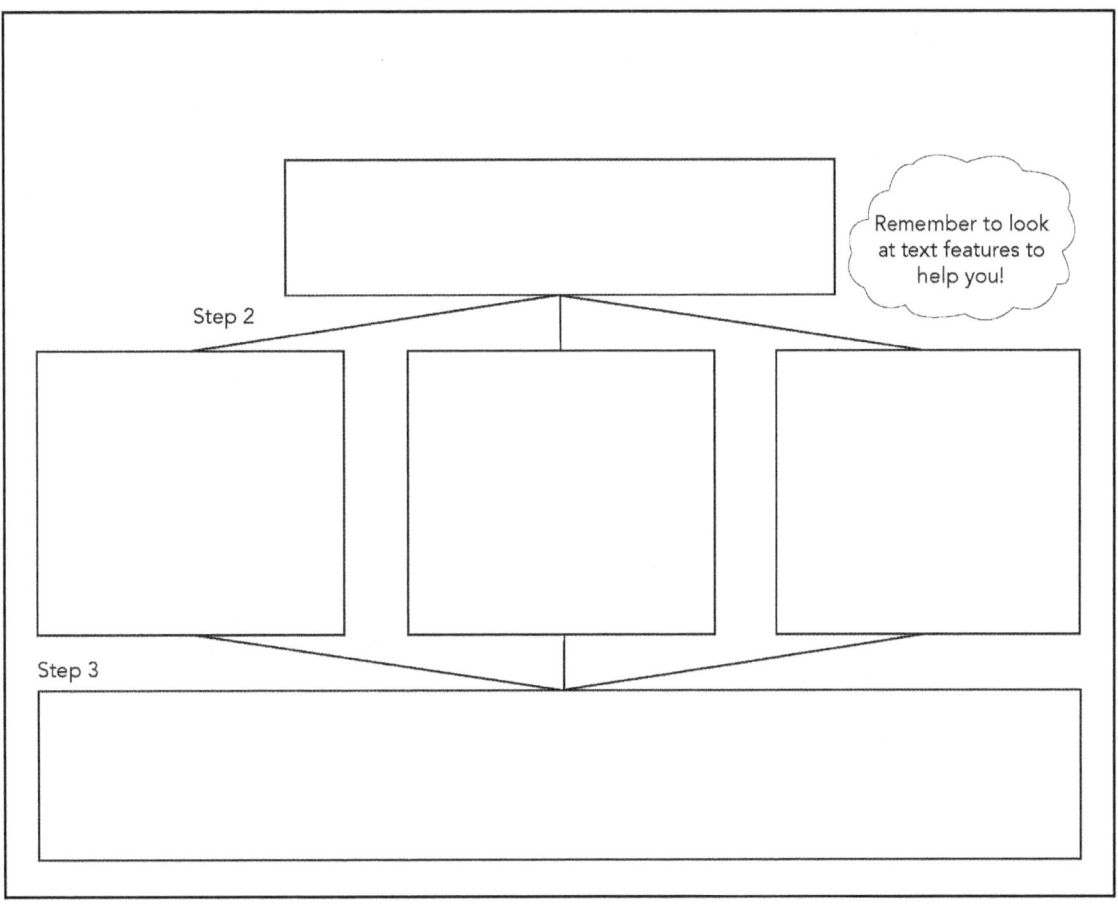

Step 2

Remember to look at text features to help you!

Step 3

Student booklets are available via the QR code at the end of the book

STUDENT BOOKLET DOWNLOAD

Purchasers of **How to Create Language Experts with Literary Terms** may use this QR code to download booklets from this book at no extra cost. This will ease the process of making copies for students and expand learning options. Both the print and digital download versions of this material are protected by copyright laws.

QR codes can be found in all LtoJ books, providing access to digital downloads of student worksheets.

ABOUT THE AUTHORS

Codi Hrouda grew up in the small town of Hubbard, Nebraska. After completing high school, Codi went on to pursue her degree in Elementary Education at Wayne State College, and graduated with a BA in Elementary Education in 2000.

Once graduated, Codi accepted her first job at Thurston Elementary School, in Thurston, Nebraska, as a fifth and sixth grade combination teacher. A year later, she and her husband moved to Columbus, Nebraska where she taught a year of first grade and then thirteen years of fourth grade at Centennial Elementary School. While teaching full-time in Columbus, she completed her master's degree in Curriculum and Instruction through Wayne State College. She graduated with her master's degree in May of 2006.

In 2014, Codi and her husband moved their family back to the area where she grew up to raise their three daughters. Codi accepted a fifth grade position at Dakota City Elementary in Dakota City, Nebraska where she continues to teach today. She just completed her twenty-second year of teaching in 2022. Codi spends her free time attending her daughters' activities, decorating, reading, and spending time with her family and friends.

Emma McInerney grew up in the small town of Elk Point, South Dakota. After completing high school, Emma went on to pursue a degree in healthcare at South Dakota State University (SDSU).

In 2015, she realized she was ready for a career change because her passion lies in education. She transferred to Dakota State University (DSU), earned a degree in Elementary Education, and graduated in 2019. Emma began her first job at Dakota City Elementary, in Dakota City, Nebraska, as a fifth grade teacher. While teaching full-time she completed her Masters degree in Curriculum and Instruction through Wayne State College, graduating in May of 2022. Emma concluded her third year of teaching in 2022, and she continues to teach alongside her co-author, Codi Hrouda.

Emma returned to her hometown of Elk Point after graduating, and spends her free time reading, gardening, and spending time with her boyfriend, family, and friends.

Dr. Lyle Lee Jenkins is an author, speaker, and recognized authority in improving educational outcomes. He believes that implementing a growth mindset and celebrating progress are the keys to helping students learn more and retain their enthusiasm for school.

His education experience, that spans over 50 years, ranges from working as a teacher, a principal, and a school superintendent in the California School System to being a University Professor. In 2003, Lyle Lee founded LtoJ, LLC hoping to impact and guide the way we approach education.

Lyle Lee Jenkins has authored six books showcasing continuous improvement in schools, including *How to Create a Perfect School*, *Optimize Your School*, *Permission to Forget*, *From Systems Thinking to Systemic Action*, *Improving Student Learning*, and *How to Create a Perfect Home School*. All literature offers powerful, practical suggestions for every aspect of education. The two most influential people supporting Dr. Jenkins's work are W. Edwards Deming and John Hattie.

Having spoken to educators all across the United States, Latin America, Europe, Australia, and Asia, Lyle Lee Jenkins is passionate about equipping the next generation with a true love of learning.

Dr. Lyle Lee Jenkins holds a Bachelor of Arts degree from Point Loma Nazarene University, a Masters of Education from San Jose State University and a Ph.D. from the Claremont Graduate University.

Lyle Lee Jenkins's website, www.LtoJ.net, is a great place to discover useful tools to guide your educational journey.

Do you have a great photo or video of your student using one of our products?

We would love the opportunity to share it on our website and social media channels!

Email us at info@ltoj.net

If you have a story to share, we would also like to hear from you. We feature student stories during presentations and on our social media accounts.

Our team loves sharing the joy of a child understanding new concepts. It allows our audience to experience firsthand the mission our team works towards every day; for students to maintain the same love of learning they brought to Kindergarten throughout all their years of schooling and into adulthood.

Thank you for being a loyal customer. We appreciate you!

The LtoJ Team

*Follow us on Instagram, Facebook, TikTok and YouTube
@LtoJLLC*